I0626428

Being Present with the Past

Jeanne T. Bartlett

FAR END PRESS

ISBN 979-8-9988997-2-0

Book cover design by Erin Kirk
Art on front and inside back covers by Thomas W. Rivers
Photographs by Esther A. Titcomb featured on opening page, as well as
    pages 10, 17, 28, 38, 55, 69, 72, and 81

Printed in the United States of America
First printing September 2025

Published by Far End Press
64 Dudley Brook Road
Deering, NH, USA 03244

AUTHOR'S NOTE

Her relentless probing, her many questions have infused my prose and poetry with just the right amount of clarity and polish. To my editor, Amanda Marsh, I am most grateful for seeing this project through with such a discerning eye.

To my writing group, past and present—Janet Barry, Sylvia Beaupré, the late Charlotte Bell, Ellen Dokton, Chris Hague, Marilyn Shaw Paul, Becky Schaefer, Margaret Seymore, Alice Thomson—and to Three or More's Melody Russell and Joan Weddle, I offer my deep appreciation for your patience, skill, and knowledge of what makes a good read. To my sister, a fine writer herself, I give my thanks for insisting: "Keep on writing." For my family who first asked, "Tell me about the Olden Days, Mom," I give my heart.

An editor for *The Weare Register* had once asked for my recollections about growing up in rural New Hampshire in the 1930s and 1940s. And so, I wrote. Turning the pages of a ragged scrapbook and reading the faded newspaper columns pasted within, I remembered the words from someone: "This should be in book form."

As I visited these columns twenty-five years later, I saw that they were in need of a bit of "spit and polish," but they still remain within the spirit and recollection of one who now has many more years between then and now, between past and present. I wrote then as a person who felt a certain way about the past and its memories, rather than as an historian. I still write that way today, as I continue *Being Present with the Past*.

CONTENTS

Old Frog Pond

One day, just the two of us carried tools to our crop of Christmas trees to clear the brush crowding their growth. We found gifts among the boughs as we worked in the spring warmth: last year's bird nest, still secure after winter's icy blasts, and a fox den cleverly hidden beneath the roots of a blue spruce. Spread about its entrance were more presents: guinea hen feathers, a mallard wing, and a long bone. Earlier that spring, I had watched a fox from my kitchen window. She carried a kit in her mouth as she trotted into the woods. She returned four more times to finish settling her family, removing kits from her den too near our road. Once, we found a dead kit that had been hit by a car, its fur still so soft and silky.

We rested on a flat rock next to the frog pond. Sweat from hard work clearing around the trees had dried, gluing shirts to shoulders. He said, "Remember the mossy bank?" I smiled, thinking about how another sort of sweat soaked the moss where we had lain. Ferns caressed my legs as I recalled those courting days. Suddenly a finch, wearing gold on gold, came to sip from the little pond. His brilliance, a shining sword piercing the forest shadows, ignited a memory from my childhood.

I told him about my hours spent beside the pool, digging a kind of clay from the bank to fashion small cups and bowls for the fairies. Eyes watched me as I put my dishes to bake on the warm rock. Did

those frogs mean to come for tea? Leaves pinned together from the mountain alder tree made wonderful placemats. I had picked wild strawberries to fill my tiny molded bowls.

Our family cow had often visited this spring-fed pond. As I looked up from my play, I could see her worn path, a narrow strip, woven in and out and around boulders littering the hillside. She would mince her way down this path, her heavy body swaying, to drink and swell her sides. With a groan, her fringe-ended tail brushing flies away, she would climb back up the hill, her bell on its leather collar sounding her approach to the barnyard. "Come boss, come boss," my father would call as he waited in the stable doorway with his milk pail, the bill on his cap turned around to the back of his head. Cream, skimmed from milk that had been sitting in wide enameled pans on a stone ledge in our cool cellar, would be so delicious on those little wild strawberries.

We returned to the field to pick up our tools—clippers, bow saw, a scythe—and made our way home through rows of fragrant young fir trees. Crossing the field toward our house, I wondered where the fox was living now.

First Run Sap and Haiku

The drill bites deep
A man and a boy
Watch the sap run

This brief poem was written after a day of hanging sap buckets. Our son worked with his father, the warm morning sun shining on his blond head as he bent to the task.

That was thirty years ago, though I remember thirty years before that—those warm days and cold nights signaling our senses. The dusty sap pails were brought into the kitchen from where they had been stored in the barn loft. This loft had become more spacious as winter wore on, the hay supply having dwindled as we fed our faithful horse and Jersey cow each day. The thrill of jumping from the barn rafters into the hay became more intense as the pile diminished. The hay dust and chaff flew in the air as I landed below from a height that seemed so dangerous.

Mother argued that it was much too early as she reluctantly turned away from her seed catalogs to scrub the buckets. Last year's calendar had to be consulted for the pencilled-in reminder of a previous tapping. We piled the pails on a sled and took them into the woods where sugar maples waited to yield their spring's rising.

My father's hand drill would turn as he leaned toward the tree, shavings sweet and moist spilling onto the snow-covered ground. The metal buckets were hung and a sound like distant gongs grew throughout the forest as the first run sap fell.

A large, shallow pan would be placed over a loose brick fireplace in the woods. There my father spent many hours emptying buckets, slipping in the snow, and keeping the fire going with wood piled high from a previous year's cutting. When the sun rose high in the sky, he took potatoes out of a burlap sack, the very smallest from the root cellar (called pig potatoes), and buried them in the coals. Later they would be forked out from the fire, and we would toss them back and forth in our mittens to cool them. Though they were sometimes black and brittle outside, we loved the flavor of their hot insides. If the sap had approached syrup stage, he would pour some out on clean snow, and that lovely sweetness peeled from the snow completed our meal. We would laugh at each other's faces blackened and sticky from our woodland picnic.

Sometimes he would boil late into the night, and standing in the stable doorway, I could see a red glow of fire. Smoke drifted above tall pines. As I turned toward the house, there was my mother framed in the window. Lamplight pooled over seed catalogs scattered about the table. Wetting her finger, she turned the pages, a pencil perched above her ear.

Cold nights, warm days
Hanging empty steel buckets
The maples sound their gongs

Easter

It was nearly Easter, though snow still banked against the house, when the woman heard a knock at the door. A man stood there asking if there were any antiques for sale. She held back the urge to close the door against his quick, appraising eyes. Eyes that took in the orphaned piglets in an egg crate behind the stove; overalls, patched on patch, drying on lines strung across the kitchen. Rubber boots, also patched, stood stiffly by the door, erect with caked mud.

His eyes slid by the long table, center of this large kitchen, where that long winter and warmth from a wood-fired cook stove kept the family close. That table where, on certain days and seasons, bread was set to rise, a butchered pig was cut up, meals were taken, and schoolwork was labored over. In summer, rows of glass canning jars cooled there. On rare leisure moments, the checkerboard would be spread out, or a Monopoly game, with all that empowering paper money.

This man's gaze rested on a highchair in the corner. It wasn't much of a chair, painted blue, over green, over yellow; chipped and chewed by new, little white teeth. Decal swans floated on its back, their tail feathers peeled away. This highchair, its tray long gone, lower rungs encrusted with remnants of food, had held several small children. An old apron tied to its arms and around their middles kept them safe. The chair's seat had a trap door, and a little pot could be slid under it.

The little chair now served as a resting place for the Sunday *Boston Globe* and a tower of empty egg cartons. Yet this dealer, noting its primitive lines and assessing the time to remove all that paint, the decals too, offered to buy it.

The woman wanted at once to say no, not that chair. *He would miss it,* she thought. He? The father. Old, yet oddly fresh resentment rose in her as she remembered the times she had sat in front of the toddler, coaxing her to eat. That little one was so thin, and her worry had deepened when her husband once sighed mournfully, "She'll never make it." Spoken, it seemed to her, as though he were discussing the fate of the runt from a pig litter. Determined, she had buried turnip and carrots in mashed potatoes to tempt the child. At this time of year, root crops were abundant, as was the cod liver oil, free from the clinic. There was no way to mask the flavor of cod liver oil. Fishy smelling drops had splattered the chair.

The woman argued with herself. After all, it wasn't as if there would be any more babies. She had been forty when the girl was born and two years later, there was a son, and even after that a stillborn. Now she thought about new shoes for the girl who was no longer thin or in danger of dying from anemia; she would be nine in April and had a part in the church program.

An agreement was made, and the woman tucked the money under a
clock on the mantle. She did not watch the dealer carry the chair to
his truck already overloaded with household items from other farms.
Standing by the window, her daughter could see a corner of an old
settee belonging to a neighbor. The man in that family had had an
infection in his arm and could not work in the woods that winter. She
saw the Putnam's crib, too; their baby had died a few weeks ago. As
the truck drove off, a bit of another neighbor's pieced quilt waved
back from the tailgate. Millie wouldn't be needing that quilt in the
County Home. As the girl turned from the window, her mother took
a sheet of newspaper, placed it on the floor and told her to stand on
it while she drew around her bare feet, making a pattern. That night,
heads close under the lamplight, she and the girl found the shoe

section in the Spring/Summer Sears catalog. It took a long, delicious time to make a choice.

The father in his chair at the other end of the kitchen, where the lamplight did not reach, smoked his pipe and thought up verses about days gone by.

The next day, the newspaper feet and a money order for two dollars went into the mailbox.

The year was 1938, and there would be other kinds of dealers at the door asking if the farm was for sale.

Mayflowering

The above definition does little to describe the heartbreaking fragrance or evocative memories that arise when one finds these little flowers here in southern New Hampshire.

A few years ago, I was shopping at a small grocery store in Hillsborough when the manager spoke from behind the counter: "Do you want to go Mayflowering?" The day was clear, a little chilly but with a sun now higher in the sky. There was promise on this fine morning. The Contoocook River was boiling under the bridge, thrashing with springtime madness. Of course, I with my long list of errands and he with his duties in the store knew that it was impossible to embark on such an adventure at that moment. Mayflower is the common name for *Epigaea repens*, and his invitation, accompanied by a big grin, brought me to mindfulness. Each of us had our own recollections of places to "Mayflower." I drove home, smiling and warmed by those memories.

My sister, eleven years my senior, had a place along a brook which she called the Arbutus Trail. She searched under fallen tree limbs for those leathery evergreen leaves sometimes intermingled with brown, uninviting leaves. There would be several visits to secret spots to gently lift the leaves in the hope of finding those shy, sweet blossoms, so often hidden from the unknowing eye. There was always a certain amount of competition at school. Who would be the first to bring these flowers to the teacher? Men cutting wood or grading the dirt roads might put down their saws or climb off their tractors to cut a few stems, and with a great gentleness, tuck them in their breast pocket to bring home.

I remember my sister's letter, after she had grown and left for the city, begging my mother to send her some Mayflower buds. We would pack them in damp moss, in a box, and mail them to her, hoping that this time, they might open on her windowsill.

Yes, I have my own special spot and must leave now to search for this elusive, springtime treasure.

> The thorny hedgehog
> safe in his body armor
> trailing arbutus

Memorial Day

As the black flies murmur in my ears, I hope I can still hear warblers calling as they pass through on the way to their trysting places up North. Failing hearing, though, there is the seeing. Apple trees in blossom, lilacs in bud.

When I was a student in the East Deering School, I would watch the lilacs and hope they would not go by before Memorial Day. This was the flower we gathered to carry to the cemetery and leave on graves of soldiers buried there. Classes suspended for the afternoon, we lined up clutching our lilacs in one hand, receiving a small American flag to hold in the other.

The day for this march to the graveyard always seemed to be hot. We started out in high spirits, perhaps even singing a chorus of the

"Battle Hymn of the Republic": *His truth is marching on / Glory! Glory! Hallelujah!* Sometimes we sang "Tenting Tonight": *Many are the hearts that are weary tonight / Wishing for the war to cease / Many are the hearts looking for the right / To see the dawn of peace / Tenting tonight, Tenting tonight / Tenting on the old campground.* Our thin reedy voices rang through the branches of ancient maples. Warriors themselves, these trees lined the roadside on our way to the cemetery. The boys managed to carry sticks, along with flowers and flags. They became soldiers battling all the way to the hilltop graveyard.

There was a curious silence as we walked between the gray leaning headstones and laid our lilacs down, sticking our flags into little iron stands or in the ground. Dire warnings whispered by the older kids about not walking on the graves, where bodies had been buried, kept me in a reverent mood.

Released at last from our solemn mission, we ran down the hill toward our ride home, the big boys kicking stones and having sword fights. I, however, had a blister on my heel and a scraped knee from an inevitable fall on the graveled road. Soon I would soak my wounds in the icy healing waters of Dudley Brook.

Gifts

For thirty years I managed the Far End shop, often referred to as "a trading post of culture and ideas." Our old barn was renovated to display American handcrafts along with goods imported from many places abroad. On buying trips I sought out unique and beautiful craft, trying to imagine what a person might want to own or give to that someone who "has everything."

Growing up, I did not have everything, and I often wondered what my father would have said about the items in my shop. A barn that had housed our horse and new calves, the loft where hay had been heaped, now held wraps and dresses hung on racks for customers.

My father, orphaned at thirteen and sent out from England to work on a farm in Quebec, did not make frivolous gift-giving a priority. When I was twelve or so, he had to put aside his farming for a time and accept a job in Lawrence, Massachusetts—that state we referred to as "away." A machinist by trade, he lived in a boarding house and took a bus to work each day. There I imagine he found the power of a steady paycheck.

My brother and I helped my mother run our little homestead, finding our own empowerment, I think. We did not have an automobile, so when my father came home on his rare visits he relied on public transportation and lots of walking. Delivery drivers were willing to give one a lift, perhaps even the mailman on his rounds might give him a ride. It was an occasion when my father arrived in his city clothes, cane and satchel in one hand, a paper bag in the other. Oddly this bag seemed to break open, and lovely bright oranges would spill and roll about the kitchen floor. This was always a nice treat for us who had had enough of the winter root crops stored in our cellar.

Once my father had a long heavy boat delivered to us. He reasoned that it would be practical for one of us to row it across Lake Horace (called the Weare Reservoir back then) to the dam area where he could likely meet our boat. One day my mother sent me running down through the woods to where our boat, hidden in the tall weeds, tied to a birch, was moored near the shore. Father had gotten a ride to Chase Village and was walking on to the Reservoir where he would wait for me. Fighting the wind, as a novice oarsman, it took much longer than I expected. As I rowed, I pictured him looking up-lake, shading the sun from his eyes with his hand, leaning on his cane.

When I finally bumped my vessel into the sandy place where he was waiting, I could see that he was tired from his walk, his travel, and that he would have little sympathy for the blisters on my hands. I cannot remember which one of us manned the oars on the way back to our cove, the wind at our back, but I still remember how to row a boat. My brother and I often launched this same boat out on the lake at dusk fishing for hornpout.

Another time he sent us a coon dog from someone he knew who was looking for a home in the country for a faithful old dog. He arrived in a crate at the railroad station in North Weare. We had never had a pet and, though I would have liked a lively puppy, I did not say so. We called this sable-colored, sad-eyed fellow, Jack. He loved us and drooled his devotion on any knee that was available to him. His wonderful baying bark was full and robust, but he hated to go out in the cold. Jack was a southern bred dog, so all the New Hampshire raccoons, which I think my father thought we would hunt, were safe.

Later, my father also sent us a bicycle, brand new and beautiful. It had a crossbar which signified that it was a boy's bike, and my brother's eager, joyful expression fell when he was told that he could carry his sister on the front bar.

The oranges, the boat, the dog, the bicycle are only memories. My father's lasting gifts remain in me as the gift of life, the gift of imagination.

August Homestead

My father's scent lingers in the old jacket still hanging in the barn—
a mixture of sweat, tobacco, axle grease, bag balm, shaving soap.
Dipping my face in the denim folds, recollections from childhood
rise and surface.

A summer day. Hot. Rumbling thunder, distant but ominous. From
my perch high atop the hay wagon I see my father's face, lifted to
scan a clear blue sky. His hat, a battered straw, thatch of dark hair
thrust through a hole, tips back for a moment, and I look into
that face, one full of will, willing it not to rain on his dry hay. His
expression mirrors the look he had when peering into our well,
worried about the dropping level of water. His heavy black mustache
still holds droplets from his drink of ginger beer. It's a brew my
mother makes out of ginger and water, then sends to the field in a
salt-glazed jug. That's one of my jobs, carrying that jug to him, to
where he works in the hot sun. The cords along his brown arms
glisten and bulge as he swings his pitchfork, heavy with hay, to the
top of our wagon.

Many years later I can still recall the view from high up on that
hay load, how my staggering gait, back and forth over hay hills
and valleys, packed the load. I could see my mother bent over the
vegetable rows in the garden bordering this hayfield; her figure
looked tiny, so diminished. Barn swallows do not collide with each

other in their sky dance, but do they see me? From this height, our horse's ears—now forward, then quickly laid back as the load gets heavier—seem far away. Her harness dark with sweat lies black against her shining rump.

There is a nest of hairless mice I want to save, but it disappears under a forkful of hay. Hay is coming faster now and with it a ribbon-like snake spinning in the air, tossed by my brother who wishes he was pitching a baseball today instead of raking hay. I hold back my hay-fright to spite him and to preserve the solemn beat of the pitchfork, respectful of my father's urgency as the thunder sounds closer. Now I wonder if he saw the sailing snake, and did he smile at the ground, not at my brother? Sweat from heat, effort, and fear makes rivers through the hay dust on my arms; the part between my braids lengthens down my back.

If supper time ever comes, there might be fresh peas, milk, and new potatoes. My mother will walk with us to the brook, the water sure to be cold but flowing slowly in the heat. My mother sits in the shallow pool, her house dress billowing around her. We, her ducklings, in our featherless skins, splash her and each other. She carries our clothes as we run still wet, up the road through the gathering dusk, our feet making mud prints on the dry sandy road. The soles of my feet, now leathery from summer use, rake through the evening grass; wet green blades sprout between my brown toes.

My father sits in his Morris chair at one end of the long kitchen. Lamps not yet lit, he watches the fireflies swirling past the window, his pipe smoke lifting, disturbing the sleepy house flies. Lightning brightens the room as my mother swats the flies pressed numbly against the ceiling. They fall on the linoleum floor and on the grain bag towel covering the pie my father will eat for breakfast after his morning chores are done.

Our stairway, steep as a ladder, leads to my attic bed. Midday sun stored there is a delight to my body, still icy from the brook. Like a puppy through with play, I am instantly asleep.

Walking the Brook

The brook has dwindled to mostly a rock bed and, as I watch the slender stream dividing and joining, going in and out, searching for passages to some faraway destination, I remember how once I waited for just such a diminished waterway when I was a child. That is when I would tell my mother that I was going to walk the brook. Boulders and rocks would have taken on new shapes without the spring torrent surging over them. Little mossy gardens and a miniature fern forest had crowned some of them, and an occasional leopard frog leaped before me, his spots glistening jewel-like in the sunlight. My bare toes clung to the rocks as I made my way downstream, stopping occasionally to test a pool. Even in late summer, the water was cold and soothing to summer blisters and scrapes.

This time of year, I would also be looking for the cardinal flower often found along the way: *Lobelia cardinalis*, a member of the bellflower family. This slender spike of intense scarlet was a delight found on the stream bank as I slipped and slid over rocks barely veiled with water. Often only a single stalk of this brilliant flower could be found, and its solitary presence matched my own being, this particular highway mine alone.

Eventually the brook would widen and deepen; my journey would take me through the woods to the road where others traveled. I had resisted picking the cardinal flower to bring to my mother, its stature so brave, blooming there alone, but blackberries hung over the sides of the road toward home. My pockets and hands were full as I passed the barn, its loft overflowing now with hay. Mother was making pies in the kitchen, and she handed me a bit of dough to fold around the berries. Soon the baked pies, including my little blackberry one, were set to cool in front of the open window, the smell of fresh baking mingling with the scent of phlox blooming by the door.

Bird Song and Rosemary

Bird song awakened me this morning. Melodies so lovely accompanied a certain anxiety as I remembered my overdue column and my editor's gentle reminder on my answering machine yesterday. But wait! Something else came creeping through my open window besides a robin's mating call. The scent of rosemary from my herb garden mingled with the beginning of another hot, humid day. Ah, yes, I yawned—for remembrance. It has been said that students in ancient Greece tucked fresh rosemary twigs behind their ears to help them retain information.

A sprig of rosemary is here behind my ear, guiding my memory of fishing for hornpout in the lake. It had been a long hot day picking bugs off potato plants in the garden. It was getting dark as my brother and I ran down the wood road carrying our fishing poles and tackle. [*Note: A wood road was a narrow road made as a homesteader accessed his wood lot to cut trees.*] My lantern swung through the shadows on the way to a hidden place where our old green rowboat was tied to a tree. We slid our wooden vessel out from tall shore grass; the water, warmed from midday sun, soothed our bare feet as we loaded our gear and pushed off, rowing out to mid-lake. Floating there in calm water, we could see only one light from a camp in the distance.

Threading earthworms onto a hook, I would often prick my finger— discomfort soon forgotten as I dropped a line into the dark waters and began to pull up slippery, shining bodies. The black, wet

 hornpout would gleam in lantern light and, as they fell splashing into the bottom of the boat, drops would sizzle on the hot kerosene lantern. Inevitably, the spike on the hornpout's fin would pierce my hand while I struggled to remove the hook from its mouth, our blood mixing, that of the fish with mine.

Plodding home through the moist forest with our catch, we dared not look too closely at gigantic shadows the swaying lantern cast about us. A thundering bullfrog's bellow added speed to our steps toward home; his voice seemed to admonish us for invading his territory.

In the morning, my mother would affix the heads of these hornpout to a chopping block with an ice pick, skin them thus and remove their innards. The thin black skin of these fish lay curled on the ground. Their forlorn heads, their spikes and whiskers, were scattered about, our three-legged barn cat sniffing the carnage. There were other times when the head of an old hen or a cranky rooster lay about this same chopping block. Mum's axe, sharp and efficient, was ready to aid her in providing food for her family. In the kitchen, she dipped the fish in a breaded mixture and fried them for breakfast.

Reading more about rosemary, I learned that Shakespeare, too, was well acquainted with its symbolism. In *Hamlet*, Ophelia strewed herbs and flowers at the feet of her mother and brother, crying out in her madness, "There's rosemary, that's for remembrance!" Perhaps Ophelia was vainly beseeching Hamlet to remember their love or maybe just clutching rosemary to calm and restore her own mind. In any case, you can see what rosemary has done for me today.

Some further notes on "wood roads"
These homemade roads evolved as trees were harvested for firewood and building. My father used a horse-drawn, rough, rugged kind of sled on runners (some farmers had old tractors or trucks for this work). During the winter, the "slack time," my father felled and limbed the trees with an axe, sawing the logs into four-foot lengths. These logs would be brought up over the snow-covered roads and trails on his horse-drawn sled to be piled in a row near the barn or in the dooryard. There they would dry through summer and be cut down to stove-wood size in late fall. Such roads form now as forest land is harvested and large tractors and skidders bring out logs to be loaded on trucks delivering them for lumber or firewood.

Watering Place

Here are your waters and your watering place.
Drink and be whole again beyond confusion.
~from Directive *by Robert Frost*

I remember the cool spring at the foot of our steep pasture. A narrow secret pool, its water reflected my hot, red face as I lay near its edge, drinking. My father kept a metal cup in a crook of a branch there. I could see the blue granite glaze of it as I rested, my breathing slowing now.

I had been reading—hiding, really, from chores yet undone. Cleats nailed to the trunk of a huge old tree aided my climb high up into the leafy arms of a maple tree near our barn. From there I could consort with swallows dipping and sailing about the field and spy on my brother as he dug for worms, his bamboo fishing pole nearby.

In the distance, our cow's bell rang as she grazed. Time passed and I was deep in chapter six of *The Swiss Family Robinson* when I heard my mother calling. That dreaded summons had come: to go after our family cow, Daisy, who had found a break in the fence. Her bell sounded so far away as I followed her track, struggling through undergrowth and prickly brambles. It seemed as though I would never get close enough to that body obstinately crashing ahead.

She would snatch a bite from some succulent, exotic green thing, toss her horns as I approached, and run off, the bell on her collar clanging infuriatingly. Either she tired or realized that it was the milking hour—a time also for her daily ration of grain—for she suddenly stopped and, docile, allowed me to snap on a lead rope and walk with her back to the barnyard.

By the spring, I dabbed at my scratched legs with a plantain leaf dipped in the cold water, cleansing my wounds and even beginning to forgive that beastly cow. My father would soon be in the stable sitting on a low stool, his cap turned around, his head resting against Daisy's sweaty flanks, beginning the evening milking. The cats, all sizes and colors, would line up at a respectful distance in the stable doorway. They waited for the stream of milk coming their way. No matter that it sometimes hit their eyes. They licked each other's fur, loving the warm milk squirted in their direction, right from the source.

Dear Daisy—I did forgive her as I thought about her cream, rising to the top of the milk pans set in the cool cellar. Soon the cream would be skimmed off and added to our supply. I would turn the handle of our wooden butter churn and listen for the change in the rhythmic sound of cream, sloshing back and forth. Soon there would be a thump indicating a state of butter. Mum would remove a plug and drain off the bluish buttermilk that my father loved to drink. The remaining substance—butter—would be pressed into a wooden one-pound measure for sale or barter. An irregular mound was kept covered in a brown glazed dish for family use.

I visit the spring, now quite overgrown. The cup is gone; my parents too.

September Harvest

The memories of summer will be stored like a squirrel's nuts;
in winter take them out and look at them one by one.
                                        ~Rumer Godden
                        A Time to Dance, No Time to Weep

Rows of canning jars, still warm from the water bath, lined up on our long kitchen table. Tomatoes, green beans, sweet relish, corn, and blueberries: the colors so beautiful and representing a certain security. My mother would wipe her face, dripping with sweat, on the corner of her apron as she stoked the wood stove on a warm day to keep the big canning kettle boiling. The bib of her apron was held up at each corner with a safety pin. What better way to store a pin? It might be needed to secure a child's diaper. More were kept handy, pinned to the window curtain.

The garden in fall was rich with the scent of rotting tomatoes, fat yellowing cucumbers—so much harvest to store, to preserve, to feed the pig. The pumpkins and Hubbard squash would wait for a while to be gathered, then carried into the house, up the steep stairs, to roll under someone's bed and stored for winter meals. The large corn patch would become smaller as stalks were cut down and thrown to the cow. Any overlooked cobs of sweet corn would be salvaged for the pigs who squealed with delight when my brother pitched them into the pigpen.

During the summer I had run down the rows measuring myself against the rising stalks. Soon they towered above my head, and the tassels of emerging corn tickled my ears as I searched for a special place where the sunlight filtered through. Now in the center of my "forest," the drying corn leaves rattled when I passed by.

Another measure of my growth, my ability, would be blueberrying where the high bush variety grew on a hill. Distant mountain peaks shimmering in July heat looked down on my mother and her friend Millie foraging for the blueberries they would later process in canning jars for jam and pie making during the winter. Now though, it felt like a holiday for me, my brother, and his friend Donnie. I would have a small bucket tied to my waist to fill with what the botanists call *Vaccinium corymbosum*. Sweet blueberries stained my lips and fingers. Mum noted that I could reach higher this year and counted the times that I emptied my bucket into a seemingly bottomless milk pail near her feet.

She had hitched up Molly, our mare, to the wagon that morning, adding a basket lunch of bread, maybe a can of sardines, a gallon jug of lemonade, along with large pails to hold the berries. Kids sat behind her buggy seat on the wagon floor, facing the graveled road, looking into billowing dust as she drove to a spot where she and

Millie had picked berries the year before. Resting after our picnic under a tree growing near an abandoned cellar hole, I dozed in the warmth and sound of the women's voices. They sat on an old quilt, their backs against an apple tree. Small green nubbins fell in the breeze, scattering about them as they talked.

Soon enough my brown leathery toes would be stuffed into shoes, school would begin, and another set of memories would gather to be stored.

A Winding Road

A winding road will be my style and a homestead in the hills.
~*H.S. Titcomb*

My father—poet, farmer, machinist—penned the above line as he sat in his lodgings, dreaming of the day he would find land, a barn, and a house of his own. He continued to add to his meager savings as he worked in Canada and across much of America.

Finding love and a wife in St. Paul, Minnesota, he brought her east. In two furnished rooms in Boston, their home, my father's longings caught mother's imagination, and they dreamed together about the farm they would find. A real home for them and the coming child.

Two years later he stood in the dooryard of a small cape-style house with attached shed and barn. Towering maples lined the road and sheltered the buildings. Maples to tap for syrup, a field to harvest hay for the horse, and forest to cut wood for warmth and cooking. The words tumbled out as he waved his arms about, wanting his wife and little girl to share in his excitement at this find—and all for six hundred dollars!

My mother, city born, wandered about, peering in the windows of this little house, trying out the pump handle on the well and finding the door to a two-holer outhouse.

Somehow, they settled themselves there in Deering, New Hampshire, in 1920. My father's "style" may have altered a bit as the years brought along the births of three more children and the accompanying responsibility. Responsibilities that the children shared as they grew.

As October approaches and tourists plan trips to view the glowing foliage in New Hampshire, I remember third grade at the East Deering School and coming home one day to find a saw rig set up. It was a hired machine run by a man with one arm. Fearfully, I covered my ears to shut out the "putt-putt" sound of that "one lunger" engine. Its blue smoke drifted and mingled with the yellow leaves falling from the apple tree in our dooryard. I stared at that vicious blade as it tore through the four-foot-long logs my father and brother had brought up the previous winter on a horse-drawn sled.

The pile of stove-length wood grew to monstrous proportions as the saw whined on. My parents would worry that there was not enough wood for warmth and cooking. I would worry about how my brother and I could possibly get all that wood thrown into the shed before snowfall. My brother would practice his aim at certain boards that framed the wood bin. Amidst flying logs, I carried in my share.

Wild roadside asters, sawdust in my shoes, and hay sticking out of a full mow are part of my October memories.

October Elephant Rocks

Late autumn leaves
the color of old blood
of rusting tractors
left to the weather
mix with shades
of burgundy, champagne

Drunk with viewing
I am a fool to think
all this will come again
For never, just this way
will I look down to find
my sneakers buried
in mounds, fallen leaves
whispering a final song

Or will I lift my face
to the slanting sun
at just this hour
Never again will I lean
to pick frost survivors
a few flowers, still so blue
and tender in my hand

~Jeanloretta

In the forest of my childhood, I'm sure I never thought about those moments as *never again* or *just this hour* when we scrambled to the top of those giant boulders we called elephant rocks. There were several of these solid beasts in our woods (one woman said that she called them ship rocks), and my brother and I would vie for certain ones: the tallest, the widest, or most lichen-covered. We rode on safari in that distant, dark continent called Africa, striking the boa constrictors that hung from the trees and shooting the lions that crouched below with our wooden weapons.

Once I visited my favorite elephant in late spring and found its back covered with tiny pink and white flowers on the ends of creeping

stems with small, round leaves. The scent from these blossoms was delicate and lovely. It was some time before I realized that they were a preview of the red partridgeberry. It took even longer for me to notice that I had not ridden on safari for a long time, that I traveled in my books and wore more dresses. I wonder if my mother noted the changes and felt a touch of sadness, or did she know about the flowering?

It would be good to ask her now, now that another fall is here.

Banking the House

Last night's sky was brilliant with stars as I tried to name the constellations in that moonless universe. The back of my neck ached with the strain of looking up, my body tending to fall before the glory of this night. Or was it simply imbalance? *When I look at your heavens, the work of your fingers, the moon and the stars . . . what are human beings that you are mindful of them . . .* (Psalm 8:3-4). That morning, I had watched leaves sailing by the window, some flattening themselves in kaleidoscope color against the panes. They seemed to be begging to come in as I washed the breakfast dishes.

This October wind raised a childhood memory of "buttoning" up our old drafty house against cold winter winds. One day I came home from school to find stakes in the ground, bracing up the long boards placed around the house foundation. There was a space between them and the house that needed to be filled. We children would take burlap grain bags into the woods where the tall pines grew. There on the ground were the pine needles, so thick that our footsteps were softened as we worked. One held the bag open while the other shoveled in the needles to fill our sacks. Back and forth between house and forest, spilling the needles into what seemed an endlessly long trench. This kept us busy until dark. More to do tomorrow, perhaps.

Sometimes I became distracted from my job and stopped to rearrange the miniature stick villages we had built under the pines last summer. Stockades, fences, houses, and barns were there; some had been demolished by an erupting mushroom. Occasionally, my brother and I would have sack races around and around tree trunks.

One night, as the moon rose, I watched its light touch long vines sprawling and twisting through the garden. Their blackened leaves took on a strange beauty, as it does, casting shadows in such moonglow. The heavy warty winter squash, pale yellow butternut, and orange pumpkins, that had been left on the vines to cure in the fall warmth for a few weeks, had been carried up our steep stairs to bedrooms. There they jostled against one another, stored under beds, during winter. I imagined them chatting with each other while I slept above them, snug in my attic bed.

At least one or two pumpkins, the largest, would be taken down to our kitchen table in late October and carved into happy or frightening faces for Halloween. Mum would save the seeds to roast; other seeds were saved for planting next year. Later those pumpkin faces were broken up and served to our pig. One day my mother would chop open one of those great hardened winter squash or cut up another pumpkin. The lovely saffron colored fruit was cooked and sometimes mixed with our cow's milk, hens' eggs, spices, and sugar, put into a pie shell to bake, and served as dessert to a growing family.

We had begun to sit under lamplight for supper as darkness descended earlier and our daylight shortened.

Our grandson, Samuel, age nine, wrote a poem about pumpkins:

THE PUMPKIN FIELD
Summer ends and fall begins, setting the alarm
Birds fly south, leaves fall, the pumpkin field does not move
People looking for a feast, take the pumpkins
Still pumpkins remain, but hungry people remain too
More pumpkins leave and soon there is only one left
The old pumpkin stays, winter comes and goes
Warm pumpkins wonder if any others are left
They go to the pumpkin field, find nothing except for seeds
They realize that more pumpkins, tons of pumpkins
are going to continue the cycle.

North Schoolhouse

The work of the eyes is done. Go now and do the
heart-work on the images imprisoned within you.
    ~Rainer Maria Rilke (as translated by Stephen Mitchell)
                             Turning Point

A skim of ice on the watering trough that lies at the foot of Peter Wood Hill reflects the early morning sun. Children climb, even run, up this very steep hill, gravel and stones spinning out from under boots and shoes as they race toward the North Deering schoolhouse.

The young teacher, who boards with a family nearby, has a goal in mind as she climbs. Just once, she hopes to arrive at the top of the hill without stopping to catch a breath midway. There may be time today to gaze out over the valley, to watch thin columns of smoke rising from farmhouse chimneys. Peter's Black Angus cattle roam the great sloping field, listlessly grazing the frost-white grass. Maples, now leafless, line the roadside, allowing a view of a small figure at the foot of the hill.

A boy has stopped to search for a firm apple among the drops on the ground beneath an old Baldwin tree growing near the stone wall, still giving up its fall crop after all these years. Some of its branches stretch far enough over the fence to where a stray black heifer has found the fallen fruit that nestles among the clumps of grass.

The boy watches the sliding to and fro of the beast's jaws as she crunches the apple, juice dripping, clouds of breath floating in the cold. A few apples still cling high up in the tree's branches. Loading a slingshot with stones, he brings them down, one by one, for the heifer who joyfully lumbers about chasing these gifts from above. Pleased with his perfect aim, he barely hears the voice of his teacher calling, "Hurry, Harold, it's time for school."

On a dead run, he scales the hill, his dinner pail swinging wildly by his side, reaching the schoolhouse before she does, in time to take his turn at ringing the bell that summons the children to class. Jump ropes, a monarch butterfly chrysalis in a canning jar, wild purple asters in a coffee can: all left by three granite steps leading up to the classroom door.

Keepsakes and Letting Go

Leaves begin to fall, old maple trees and tender saplings alike—all letting go. Why can't I let go of a child's second grade Thanksgiving drawing, turkeys roosting in trees and pilgrims praying, or those baby teeth rolling around in my jewelry box? Listen to how one woman describes the conflict she faces each time she comes across her mother's umbrella in storage: *I don't know why I'm saving it. It's old and dirty and torn, and yet I've taken it with me each time I've moved. It's been over twenty years since my mother died, yet I can't seem to throw it out. A few times already, I have held it over the dumpster, ready to drop it in, but I wasn't able to. It's crazy, because I never look at it, except when I go to get something else out of storage and there it is. Then I pick it up and look at it and can see my mother walking along with it like it was yesterday. She was never without it. I go through this debate repeatedly: Should I keep it or throw it away?*

My mother's clothes wringer is in my collection of unused items. Its rollers are cracked and the blue letters across the top are faded, barely discernible: *Atlantic Wringer Co. Universal.* There are two horseshoes on either side and the words *Good Luck.* Mum probably hoped to receive that promise as she scrubbed away on her washboard. This wringer would be clamped on to the edge of a galvanized washtub, and clothes would be fed between the rollers, the handle turned by a reluctant child. "Use both hands," she would advise as I struggled with the heavier clothes—buckles and buttons stopping progress. Again and again, she would reposition them for me. Then there would be the rinsing and the wringing once more. Washday seemed to take all day, and sometimes she would be pinning clothes on the line by moonlight.

And what about the butter churn? It also lies idle in my house. It held a potted lily one Easter and later served as a doorstop against a summer breeze. If I lift the cover today, I can still detect the faint scent of cream. There also, I was positioned at a handle, where I turned and turned, waiting for the thud sound when cream had turned to butter. Echoing, it fell from the wooden blades going round and round. Mum would sometimes pack the butter into a wooden mold; its lovely carvings inside would leave a pretty design on top of the butter after it was unmolded.

Several years ago, Heritage Day was held on the Deering Community Church grounds. We called it "Work and Play of Long Ago." Our old butter churn and the wringer were enthusiastically put into motion, little arms and hands vying for a turn. We made a pound of butter and the clothesline, strung between two trees, was full of garments from the washtub.

A wise person has said, "Over time, our need to call up memories of someone wanes, but we resist the waning as if it is a disloyalty and not a slow process of yielding. Saving a keepsake becomes a refusal to yield." Perhaps one day I will yield to letting go. Maybe if one of my five children reads this, they would like a doorstop for their home.

Taking a Walk

As I prepared this month's column, sources were reporting that the meteor display could be the most spectacular of the year as the Leonid meteors stream across the sky on November seventeenth and eighteenth. A starry night reminds me of walking on dark country roads, a darkness not illumined by streetlamps or even the brightness of electricity shining out from the houses or barns I passed on my way home from a movie in Hillsborough.

Going to the movies was a rare event, and walking to town and back was an adventure for me and my companions. Sometimes we could see a gray head through a window reading by oil lamp or a figure in denim overalls, swinging a lantern, passing from house to barn, perhaps to check on a pregnant cow long overdue.

Gene Autry rushing to rescue the rodeo from a fire set by that badman Stag Johnson in a 1942 film, *Bells of Capistrano*, still rang in my head as we trudged along the gravel road home from the movie theatre. Stopping from time to time to listen for sounds coming from behind old stone walls, we imagined an outlaw lurking behind the trees. One of us would secretly pocket a stone to toss into the darkness to scare the other. Once, the broad wingspan of an owl burst out above our heads, adding just the right amount of heart-stopping fear.

In 1943, there was no public transportation for students ready for high school. No yellow rattling buses made stops and starts in Deering to pick up children who wanted to continue their public education. Our designated school of higher learning was in Hillsborough, nearly ten miles from my home. My mother made inquiries into the availability of homes and farms where a young person could live within walking distance of the school. Most weekends and after school, one was expected to help the host family with housework, childcare, or farm chores to cover one's room and board. On one of my free weekends, I set out early Saturday morning to walk home, wanting to see Mum and my younger brother. It had snowed heavily the night before; the back road in Deering—my shortest route—had not been plowed yet. I sank up to my hips in some of the drifts before reaching home in late afternoon.

Walking was a common form of travel. My mother's friends would walk to visit with her. Sometimes a woman would have to take shelter in a vacant schoolhouse or barn until a thunderstorm passed. Another Deering woman we called Nell would stop in and amaze us when she said she was on her way to Goffstown or Manchester, always on foot. Surely, an overnight with a friend or relative would be included on those long journeys. My mother wondered if Nell had left word with her husband as to her whereabouts.

During one of my high school semesters, I lived at home and walked two miles each day to catch a ride with another student who had a car. It would still be dark, the stars pale in the sky, when I left the kitchen where I had dressed in front of the stove, oven door open for warmth. As I walked along on those early mornings, I could look out over the valley and see a single light and a thin column of smoke rising above the trees. My home lay there as solid as the stone walls I passed along the road. I longed to go back, be safe and warm, but my feet took me forward on into life.

Do Without

USE IT UP
WEAR IT OUT
MAKE DO
OR DO WITHOUT

This advice on frugality has been attributed to the Scots (or perhaps to the Amish) and has become a matter of survival for some, but also a source of amusement—even outright anger—for others. I do find it so hard to let water run from the faucet unnecessarily or throw away the smallest leftover from meals when it could be used in a soup on another day. My family was spared my various mixtures when we could feed leftovers to the pig and chickens we were raising. Our barn is empty of critters now, and I look to the compost heap to accept my offerings of food "too small to save."

Digging around in an old homestead dump, one can find very little evidence of reckless disposal. Treasure hunters love to find blue *Vick's VapoRub* jars or the lovely amber shape of an old *Watkin's Vanilla* bottle. I found a button once, buried in the dirt, that must have escaped the button jar where they were usually saved. I have been known to cut buttons off a worn shirt before tearing it up into rags, adding more buttons to my own collection in an old peanut butter jar. Rag bags: does anyone have them now or do they just buy sponges? I have seen my husband standing by our car with the hood up, one of these rags wrapped around a sparkplug or his bleeding finger. I am haunted by vague admonitions from somewhere when I dispose of things, even an egg carton. I am fascinated by all those little compartments where I could store the beads of a broken necklace I plan to restring. At least I can recycle the egg box to a hen farmer or the paper bin at our transfer station.

Finding that old button in the family dump helped me remember how my mother would substitute the buttons on cotton dresses to disguise their identity. There was a time when rural families were offered new clothes through the WPA (Works Progress Administration, which was an American New Deal agency that employed millions of jobseekers to carry out public works projects during the Depression years). The original buttons on all these shirts and dresses were a dead giveaway, always the same style, just different colors. Now, I question my mother's motives. Was she embarrassed to receive these goods? Was there some sort of stigma to getting help during those trying times?

Mum cut up or cut down used wool coats, sent on to her by a more affluent relative, to make warm jackets for the children in our house. Scraps were used to hook rag rugs. When we sorted potatoes grown and dug up in our field, some were judged too small to store in the cellar for the family's use. Sizing-up decisions were hard as we put away the little spuds to save and cook up for the pig. One woman

I know of would whisper to her children as they worked in their field unearthing these little "pig" potatoes, "Just throw them over the wall." That's how she dealt with those decisions. Today, in the markets I see bagged-up sacks of small potatoes labeled gourmet and very expensive! I whisper to myself, "Pig potatoes."

Meanwhile, I keep secret my compulsion to pick up bent nails after my husband's building projects. I want to store them in an empty coffee can and in the winter when there's quiet time, I could find a sawed-off piece of wooden plank and with a hammer straighten nails. Now that my secret is out, I might hear, "It just isn't worth your time."

Probably my adult children are among those who are amused—even annoyed—over my need to save, to store, to use up, or do without, but just the other day I found one of my daughters hanging wet laundry on a wooden rack in the cellar. I heard her husband remark, "I thought we bought a clothes dryer!"

About Pigs

This writing business. Pencils and what-not. Over-rated,
if you ask me. Silly stuff. Nothing in it.

~*Eeyore*
Winnie-the-Pooh *by A. A. Milne*

This memory of the past is something to me. I hope you will not find
it *nothing* as it unwinds. It's about pigs. They were much a part of my
growing up on our little farm. There were anxious hours near a sow's
birthing, especially. My father or mother would try to be present
when the sow popped out pink miniature likenesses, her everyday
grunts taking on a new tone, her long body rippling as she strained.
Counting at least a dozen or more, the farmer must watch the sow
to prevent her from unconcernedly sitting or rolling on her piglets
or dining on one or two. Sometimes a pig was just plain unsuited for
motherhood, so intervention took place to halt domestic violence. All
or part of the new litter might be brought into the house and bedded
down in a box behind our kitchen stove. My mother would hold
these little pigs and try to feed them a formula through a bottle with
a nipple. I don't know if she sought the advice of a veterinarian but
surely neighbors offered suggestions built on their own experiences.

I knew better than to make pets of farm animals, for they had a
destiny that did not include a long life or enduring attachments.
Nevertheless, I did learn to love one of these kitchen survivors. He
grew well and tall enough for my hand to rest comfortably on his

back as we walked side by side around the summer barnyard. His hair stiff under my touch, his skin shuddering with delight at a good scratch on his back just beyond the curl of his tail.

December brought on thoughts of Christmas to many, my family as well, but it was also butchering time. For a farm without refrigeration, the onset of winter and constant cold temperatures made it an appropriate time for the slaughtering. Men would come to help my father with this task, unrolling knives from cloth cases, testing the edge of sharp blades against callused thumbs, some fortifying themselves with home brew.

My mother cautioned me to stay in the house. Yet I heard the squeal of betrayal from my unfortunate pig and the silence after the roar of gunshot. Water boiled and boiled. The kitchen table held enough internal organs to satisfy an anatomy classroom. The hog's head with its lovely, shapely ears forward, sightless eyes fringed with white lashes, and that round wrinkled snout was brought in to sit on the table too. My mother would eventually make something called "head cheese."

The remaining carcass would be hauled up high in the rafters of the shed with a block and tackle and there it would cure. Trips to get water from the pump or armloads of firewood and outhouse visits took me by this white hairless body getting stiffer and harder as the days passed.

One dark evening, not bothering with a lantern, being acustomed to the dim shapes of familiar doorways, latches, and beams, l ran hurriedly to fill a pail from the well. I connected squarely with an unyielding object which knocked me to the rough planked floor directly beneath the slightly swaying body of . . . not my pet, not even a pig . . . but frozen pork! The fallen empty water pail rolled and echoed in the darkness. Dazed and embarrassed about forgetting this recent presence in our shed, I lay crying softly, barely making out four dainty hooves hovering above me.

December memories include more than pigs. There was the sound of click-clacking from my mother's treadle sewing machine late in the night as Christmas drew near. There was the search in a neighbor's forest for a fragrant balsam fir tree with space between its branches to safely light the little white candles in their silver clip-on holders. We stood there for our allotted ten minutes watching the light brighten my German grandfather's carved peach stones, made into tiny baskets hung with red thread; nearby a tiny bird's nest perched, the one we found in the woods that day on a bough. Soon the candles would be blown out, and we would wait for another lighting tomorrow night. The parlor was cool as only the kitchen range gave its heat to the downstairs. On Christmas day, the scent of roasting pork and baked apples would fill the house.

Once I had a pet pig
Who walked beside me
My hand on her back
A curly tail for all to see
My love for her was very big!

Henniker Story

The "Only Henniker on Earth" is a truthful claim that is fun to evoke about a neighboring town's name. When I was a little girl, a trip to Henniker by horse and buggy was rather like a trip around the world to me. My mother would sometimes buy a special cold cut in a store in town. Today my brother and I argue about what it was: I say it was liverwurst and he says it was pimento loaf. In any case, I'm sure we agree that we used to call it "Henniker meat" and that it was a special treat.

My memory of these journeys brings up a vision of looking down from our perch on the wagon seat and watching our faithful horse inching down a long, steep grade holding back the buggy and passengers, her rump rising high in her effort. Sometimes my mother stepped down from the buggy and led her down the steepest part of the road, all the while murmuring encouraging words to her and to us, my brother and me, as we clutched the rails and each other. Wild asters and dusty ferns brushed the wagon wheels; small stones rang against horseshoes and skittered into the ditches; a clear, blue sky rose over the tops of towering maples lining the gravel road.

One bright March day, years later, I stopped to watch maple syrup come to a boil at my eldest brother's farm. He stood in the sap house door, a cloud of steam rising behind him from the sap pan set over a wood fire. Mist clung to his gray hair and on the hairs in his ears sticking out from the sides of his wool cap. He leaned against the worn, sun-reddened boards covering the sides of the little house as we talked outside in the warm spring sunshine, our boots sinking into the softening snow. I told him about the piece I was writing for a column in *The Weare Register* about Henniker and my memories of horse and buggy days. He nodded and began to draw out a long-stored memory of his own. It goes like this:

There was a time when mother did not get out of the buggy on this trip. Snow lay in patches on the ground that day when she hitched up Molly, the horse, and bundled two small children into the wagon and headed for Henniker where a doctor lived and practiced. She was worried about the swelling in her leg. She did not stop to shop this time, for the doctor was stern with his advice to go home and stay off her leg and rest. She visited a family in Weare on the way home to ask for the help of a daughter there. No one was available at that time, so she and the children wound their way home. The kitchen was chilly when they got there, and the father banged the covers on the cook stove, stoking the fire, only half hearing about the doctor's orders. It was hard for him to manage without her being up and about. In his worry and discouragement, he slammed the door on his way to the barn for evening chores.

The eldest boy, just home from school, leaned over his mother as she lay on the kitchen cot with her leg propped up on a pillow. The two younger children played nearby, suddenly very quiet while their mother wept. This boy, ten years old, gathered up some empty canning jars, filled them with snow and carefully packed them around his mother's swollen leg. He refilled these jars, emptying the melted snow into the pots of geraniums blooming on the windowsill. Two weeks passed while he tended his mother, played checkers with the little girl, and rescued toy trucks for his little brother.

Back at school he answered his curious classmates who wondered how he dared stay away from school. "I was needed at home to take care of my mother," he told them.

The teacher, in her wisdom, did not ask for further details but rested her hands on his shoulders which had already broadened, it seemed.

Wreath Making

I read this in an article about aromatherapy: *The sense of smell is powerful because it is immediately connected to the limbic system of the brain, which controls the emotions and other basic functions.* I can certainly attest to the effect that the scent of balsam has on my memory as I fill a basket with fresh evergreen boughs today. I remember a time long ago when our farmhouse kitchen floor and table were strewn with fir branches and princess pine.

Right after Thanksgiving, often earlier, my mother Bertha and her neighbors, Millie and Betty, would go into the woods with their children to gather greens to make wreaths and roping to sell in the city for the Christmas season. We would stuff boughs into burlap sacks and load a 1934 Ford following us down a wood road. The branches would prick my hands and I whined often, complaining that, surely, we had enough by now. I was urged on, for many loads were needed to fill orders from florists and stores in the city. We searched for pinecones and red berries to add to our supplies as well.

Our shed began to fill with stacks of wreaths ready for the market. The women would talk about the prices they had been offered: twenty-five cents for a small wreath, thirty-five for a large one. Their fingers grew stained with pitch, and when they stopped long enough to knead their bread or roll out pie crusts, little stains sometimes transferred to baked goods. My friend told me about finding fir needles in the sugar bowl, and when he felt a cold coming on, his mom, Millie, would apply Vick's VapoRub to his chest—pine remnants sticking to his skin. I found some in my shoes and in my sandwich at school. A fairy tale, from the Harz Mountains in Germany, said that a woman boiled pine needles to make a green tea for her husband who was deathly ill. He leaped out of bed a well man! This story greatly relieved my mind as these green bits crept into our daily bread.

The valiant Ford toiled on to the Manchester stores where as many as seven hundred wreaths were delivered, along with yards and yards of evergreen garlands, to decorate the entire front of a large department store on Elm Street. We were glad to get these orders; this income added to the "butter and egg money" kept in a blue teapot on our shelf. Christmas came to our household and so did a certain feeling of pride for my contribution to the effort that day in the woods, gathering the tips of fragrant balsam with the other women and children.

The Native American Black Elk was an Oglala Lakota holy man or shaman, who said the power of the world always works in circles. Millie's son goes into the woods gathering greens each year and has even taught his children and grandchildren how to make a wreath—the power of a circle.

Skating Memories

"Look, you can just open your coat and sail down the lake." The wind blew a mist of ice particles into the air as my husband, so graceful on the ice, drew circles around me. There I stood, laced up in my new white figure skates—a tottering figure-skater-never-to-be.

1939, the day after Christmas: my friend called to compare notes about what we had found under the tree. We had both hoped for skates. "Yes," I said, not wanting to tell her about the clamp skate variety I had unwrapped. Dreading her answer, I had to ask, "Shoe skates?" "Yes, white figure skates," she told me. Jealousy and a certain shame surged; compassion boiled in a mix of feelings. Mum had probably chosen my skates from the Sears, Roebuck & Company catalog, the price fitting her earnings made from balsam wreaths— those dozens she had made to sell in the Manchester stores. My skates never really stayed fixed to my boots, as promised by the picture found in the ever-present Wish Book. They would not glide; ankles turned over. My fingers numb in the cold tried to refasten them again and again. Then it snowed for days. Ice stayed buried long enough to help me forget my dreams of figure skating.

Last night I lay on the couch watching the PBS program *Victoria*. There was a skating scene where the queen as a young woman glided gracefully over the ice, followed by laughing children in a snaking line. Her lovely husband, Prince Albert, skated and pushed the youngest in a beautiful little chariot on runners. How effortlessly they all flew around the little pond, she in voluminous skirts, snowflakes swirling about her velvet bonnet. I just had to wonder: shoe skates or clamp skates?

Two servants watched from a sleigh piled with blankets. A pair of horses in their traces stamped their feet as they waited beside the pond.

A raven family
watches the steaming dung and
the horses' breath-clouds

January

On New Year's Day, 1998, I was walking along a road at dusk seeing Jupiter close to a sliver of moon in the southwest sky. A renewing moon in a new year can cause one to reflect on things like wisdom and growth. Christian history tells us that the three wise men finally arrived at the site of a special birth on the twelfth day of Christmas. Trusting a star, they traveled over moor and mountain inquiring here and there, reassuring themselves that this journey was important and necessary in their role as wise men.

It was the winter of 1941 and I was twelve when I got a check from the Town Highway Department in Deering for my work at shoveling snow. There had been a furious blizzard, and the wind-driven snow covered the stone walls, joining one field to another in an unending white landscape. The town's snowplow—a gigantic, noisy McCormick—struggled to plow even a narrow passageway as snow continued to drift across the road. Several of us had responded to the call to dig a path ahead of the plow in the middle of a road we hardly recognized anymore. The wind continued to blow the fine snow into drifts, and my companions were only dark shapes as I looked back at the ragged line of figures, bending and raising shovels in a strange sort of rhythm.

From time to time, we would be invited into the warm kitchen at a farmhouse nearby to have a rest. Stamping snow from our boots, our faces radiant from effort, excitement, and importance, our icy mittens clutched the proffered hot drink. During the previous fall, we had gathered in this same house for oyster stew after the husking bee held in their barn across the road. I remembered this as I stood by their wood stove, snow melt from my collar trickling down inside my coat.

The Loveren family had had a good harvest. Ears of corn made a mountainous heap that stretched from end to end across the spacious barn floor. Neighbors, friends, and family members sat on rough plank benches on either side of the long row, stripping husks from the corn. Apparently when the silk is stripped away, it prevents rot in ears stored throughout the long winter. When a rare red ear of corn appeared, there was a shout, then a hush, for it was a signal to allow the holder of this prize to give someone a kiss. There were roars of laughter which frightened me somewhat. Our parents appeared strange and foolish to us as they joked and gossiped, forgetting the hardships of the lingering Depression for one evening. Nearby in a stanchion, a cow lowed, puzzled by the commotion. A baby stirred in his basket nested in a pile of corn husks, and a toddler suddenly peeped out from his own mountain of husks. The scent of kerosene from lanterns carefully hung on nails above our heads; a faint smell of whiskey emanating from a man as he bent to lift a crate of corncobs; sweet fragrance from the evening milking: all blend together in my memory of that festive night.

The stars did eventually come out after that snowstorm, bringing along a measure of reassurance to the world. A world where my small contribution to it felt very large.

ICICLE
weeps
in
the
sun
l
i
g
h
t

l
e
n
g
t
h
e
n
s
.
.
.
.
.
.
.

Midwinter

In the bleak midwinter, frosty wind made moan,
Earth stood hard as iron, water like a stone;
Snow had fallen, snow on snow, snow on snow;
In the bleak midwinter, long ago.
~*Christina Rosetti*

These lines and the harmony of this nineteenth-century hymn rang
in my head as I drove home from choir practice at the Deering
Community Church. In the clear moonless night, Orion stood
brilliant over the bare, far-reaching branches of maples lining the
road. Beginning in late fall, this giant constellation had been making
its silent way from out of the west to stand in the east in all its mighty
splendor. Orion at its post, *snow on snow*, wood smoke hanging in the
air, reminded me of winters more than half a century ago.

Earth did feel *hard as iron* as I helped my mother hang out the
laundry, which had become nearly clean on a scrub board propped
in a galvanized wash tub where a big irregular chunk of yellow soap
floated. Often, that soap would slip from my mother's reddened
hands as she scrubbed, and she would search for it among the
overalls and socks. Some of the dirtier chore clothes had been heated,
pushed about in an oblong copper vessel full of water steaming on
the cook stove. A wringer, fastened to the center of a stand which
also held a tub of rinse water, squeezed out water as the handle was
turned. *Frosty wind* bit my fingers and soon froze the clothes pinned
on a clothesline stretched between weathered posts in our yard.

Even after a few days outside, heavier items still refused to flap in the wind. I remember walking my father's union suit, stiff and tall, towering above my head, up the path and into the kitchen, where it abruptly bent in two in the warmth.

Suddenly, it seemed, we would hear the dripping of snow melting off the roof eaves, and men could be seen leaning against assorted vehicles in the sun and talking about the January thaw. My father would hitch up Molly, our Morgan mare, to a crude sled and bring up some of the long lengths of wood he had cut during slack winter times. If we were quick, we kids would catch a ride on the back of his sled, dragging our feet, our overshoes making furrows in the snow.

The flavor of a bright orange found in the toe of our Christmas stockings was only a memory, but there was a new lard supply freshly rendered from the pig. My mother made lovely pies: apple from the Baldwin crop, blueberry from jars canned last summer, and custard when our hens were productive.

Just as suddenly, temperatures would drop and *water like a stone* became a constant. Children arrived for school, noses running, faces ruddy from the cold outdoors. We were permitted to leave our accustomed row of desks for a time, to ring about the stove at the front of the room. The scent of cow barns, moth balls, a slight skunk smell from some boy's trapping experience, and wet wool from

mittens and hats drying by the stove filled the air. Often, I would become drowsy as I listened to the murmuring first graders, grouped in a corner, reading aloud. Our teacher overlooked sleeping students as she grappled with a schedule of lessons encompassing all eight grades. She even dispensed spoonfuls of cod liver oil to each child during a time when there was a mandated rural Children's Health Plan in place.

At home during moonlit nights, never worrying about traffic (everyone we knew was home where they belonged), we slid down dirt roads on our sleds at terrifying speeds, sparks flying from beneath the runners gliding over stones poking up from the ice-glazed road. My brother hoped to coast a full mile before he stopped. Home again, ice clung to our buckled boots, which we kicked off in the kitchen, clods of snow hissing against the stove. There was pie and soon we tumbled into our cold beds, Orion standing guard in the sky.

Moving On—2000

When the wrenching decision to make a change in our living arrangements arrived, we entered the realm of negotiation and appraisal involving the housing market. A realtor asked us to provide a complete description of our property for sale. Listing acreage bordering a lake, a Christmas tree grove, our six-bedroom house, barns, and garage was the obvious. As I began to describe our offering, I started to question what a complete description should look like. How complete is complete?

In a fit of passion, I began to write an addendum: I must also tell you about the beautiful winter sunrises from the east windows; about Bertha's pine, viewed from the loft in the barn, where the crow sentinel sits watching his family feeding; soothing sounds from a brook on an early spring evening—day's work done; the elephant rock in the woods that has partridge berries growing on its back; or a place where ice age boulders tumbled together to create a cave; the fox den under the fir tree where egg shells and guinea hen feathers laid about its door; how the foxes barked at us from a hollow place along the path to the lake; how we lay in the field to watch the meteor showers one dark night; that a great blue heron swings by each day overhead greeting us with his deep "Auk"; fishing by lantern light, mosquitoes humming all around; or about the early arrival of wild flowers—the sweet scent of mayflowers found in secret places along a wood road, the pink blush of lady slippers blooming under pines;

how a friendly young beaver splashed and spanked his tail at us when we came to swim by the dock—that is how to be complete.

Yes, someone did buy our home and land eventually, and I hope they find life there complete in some measure. We have moved to a smaller place nearby and closer to the brook that fairly roars now as it breaks the bonds of snow and ice that have muffled its song. We delight in the witnessing and the listening.

I have not seen fox, but an otter has been spotted on the opposite bank of the river. I have had to wait for birds to appear at feeders which remained full for over a month. One day a chickadee "scout" approached, and within an hour several species of birds landed to investigate the seed bounty.

Patience expended waiting for the brook to open and birds to appear evaporated as I searched for picture hooks, coffee filters, the top to a sugar bowl, and the hammer. So many of our sentences began with "Have you seen . . . ?"

Letting go, resettling, takes its toll, but I find surprise and joy in discovery. Tips from spring bulbs spike through leaves banked against a stone wall. Someone else planted them long ago. We are here to watch and wait.

ABOUT THE AUTHOR

Jeanne Bartlett was born in 1929, joining three other siblings, and raised on a small homestead in New Hampshire. Poetry filtered throughout her family, both written and recited, and stayed with her through high school in Hillsborough, NH, and Lawrence, MA, and after: during nurses training at Tewksbury State Hospital, marriage in Lowell, MA, ensuing motherhood, and then back to NH to live on the land of her birth. She helped her husband raise their five children and opened a handmade craft and import shop in an old barn, called The Far End of Deering (and the near end of Weare). Travels took her to NYC; Mexico; Cornwall, UK for jazz; Paris; and house sitting in New Mexico for a year or so. In between, you might have seen her at 4H pony, sheep, or cow shows with the kids, or in Casco Bay, ME, and beyond, on the ocean under sail with her husband. Maybe you saw her, or heard her, during these past sixty years, attending poetry classes, workshops, retreats, and a writing group. Once she and her husband sang in *Aida* with the Surry Opera Company in Maine, but more often she was found singing with the Deering Community Church choir. She now believes that she has found her truest voice, coming through the process of writing prose and poetry.

Jeanloretta (her stage name) reads and writes,
living just down the road from where it all began.

www.ingramcontent.com/pod-product-compliance
Lightning Source LLC
Chambersburg PA
CBHW051652120626
46551CB00015B/2329